Meet the Author

Judy Palmer has a long history of designing and publishing macramé instruction books. Her first book was published in 1978 when the macramé craze was just beginning and followed by 13 more books through the mid-80's.

Judy rekindled her passion for knotting in 1999 when she teamed up with Grace Publications to author a new bestseller, <u>Hang It Up with Macramé</u>. A second title, now out of print, was released the following year. This current collection continues to offer Judy's wonderful designs, simple instructions and detailed diagrams for your knotting pleasure.

Judy owned a family craft store for 25 years in Bloomington, Indiana. She now works for the Indiana University Student Foundation and is a free-lance designer and author in her spare time.

DISCLAIMER: All patterns in this book are tested thoroughly; however, since the final outcome depends upon the size of cord used and how tightly or loosely you tie your knots, the author cannot assume responsibility for variations in individual interpretations of knots, patterns and techniques in these designs.

Product Sources

Braided polypropylene cords

PEPPERELL BRAIDING COMPANY
22 Lowell Street
Pepperell, MA 01463
978-433-2133
www.macramesuperstore.com

WELLINGTON LEISURE PRODUCTS
Craft Division
1140 Monticello Road
P.O. Box 244
Madison, Georgia 30650

G & G HANDCRAFTS
R.R. #2
Belleville, Ontario Canada K8N 4Z2
613-968-4221

Natural jute cord

DECORATOR & CRAFT CORPORATION
428 S. Zelta Street
Wichita, KS 67207
www.dcccrafts.com

Braided polypropylene, natural jute cord & wood beads

DARICE INC.
21160 Drake Road
Strongsville, Ohio 44136
www.darice.com

2mm waxed braided cotton cord

PEPPERELL BRAIDING COMPANY
22 Lowell Street
Pepperell, MA 01463
www.macramesuperstore.com

Thick 2" silver metal rings *(for belts)*

Home improvement stores or hardware stores

19" Glass circle table top for hanging table

Discount stores, home improvement stores or glass companies

A special thank you to Dixie Glass of Johnson City, Tennessee, for supplying the glass table top pictured on the front cover.

Indigo House ™ is a trademark of Grace Publications LLC

Visit us online at
www.indigohouse.com

Knotting Terms

Alternating Cords - Forming new groups of cords by taking half of the group from one previous knot and the other half from an adjacent previous knot, then tying a new knot that falls below and between those from which the cords were taken.

Anchor Cord or Ring - The cord or ring onto which double half hitches are tied.

Bundle Cords - Roll single cords or groups of cords into small bundles or balls and secure them with a rubber band for easier knotting.

Exchanging Cords - Swapping the position of knotting cords and filler cords so that the previous filler cords become the new knotting cords and the previous knotting cords now become the filler cords.

Filler Cords - Center cords that knotting cords are tied around.

Fusing Polypropylene Cords - Secure polypropylene cords by holding a butane lighter flame near them to melt the fibers together.

> *DO NOT touch the flame to the cords as it could ignite and cause severe burns. Press the side of the lighter or another tool against the melted cords to smooth them. Do not allow children to attempt this procedure.*

> *DO NOT try to fuse natural jute fibers, as they will burn. Instead knot, glue, or tape them.*

Holding Cord - The cord onto which vertical lark's head knots, horizontal lark's head knots and reverse lark's head knots are tied.

Knotting Board (or Macramé Board) - Usually a 12" x 18" fiber board with a printed grid in 1" squares on both sides. Generally comes with T-pins to stick through the macramé work to hold it in place while knotting. Placing the pins at an angle in the board increases their sturdiness.

Knotting Cords - Right and left side cords that tie knots over filler cords, holding cords or anchor cords.

Picot - Small loops created by extending working or knotting cords at a distance beyond the original knots, then pushing them up on the filler cords next to the previous square knot.

Row - A line of adjacent knots, side by side, each tied with different working cords.

Sinnet - A continuous vertical row of knots, all of the same type, tied with the same group of working cords.

Working Cords - All cords used in the design - both those which do the actual tying *(knotting cords)* and those around which knots are tied *(filler cords)*.

Wrapping Cord - The cord used to gather and wrap a group of cords together.

GENERAL KNOTTING SECTION

LARK'S HEAD KNOT

SINGLE CORD OVERHAND KNOT
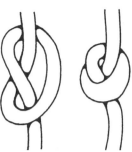

MULTIPLE CORD OVERHAND KNOT

FINISHING CORD ENDS

With an Overhand Knot

With a bead and an Overhand Knot

SQUARE KNOT IN 4 EASY STEPS

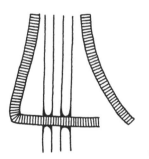 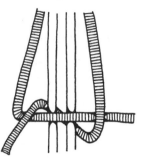 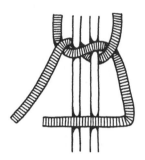 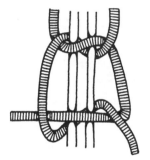

1. Make a 4 with the left hand cord.

2. Take the right hand cord over the crossbar, under the 2 center filler cords and up through the 4. This is a Half Knot.

3. Make a backwards 4 with the right hand cord.

4. Take the left hand cord over the crossbar, under the 2 center filler cords and up through the 4.

LEFT HAND SQUARE KNOT
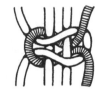

RIGHT HAND SQUARE KNOT

ALTERNATING SQUARE KNOTS
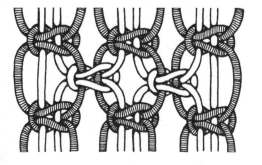

HALF KNOT
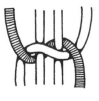

HALF KNOT TWIST SINNET

SQUARE KNOT SINNET

SQUARE KNOT PICOT
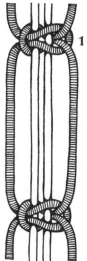

1. Make the second square knot a distance beyond the original knot.

2. Push the second knot up close to the first knot to form Picot.

HORIZONTAL DOUBLE HALF HITCH

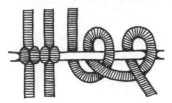

RIGHT DIAGONAL DOUBLE HALF HITCH

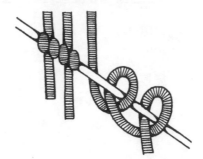

LEFT DIAGONAL DOUBLE HALF HITCH

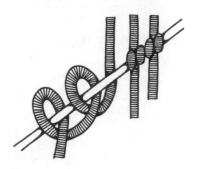

SQUARE KNOT BUTTON

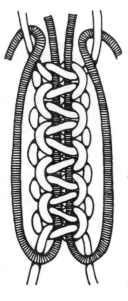
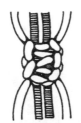

1. Tie several square knots over filler cord.

2. Thread filler cords thru working cords as shown at top of square knot sinnet & pull sinnet into a button.

3. Tie a square knot directly under button to hold it in place.

SQUARE KNOT HANGING LOOP

center ➞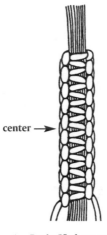
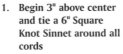
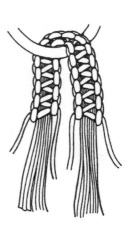
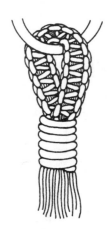

1. Begin 3" above center and tie a 6" Square Knot Sinnet around all cords

2. Center the loop through ring.

3. Tie gathering wrap around all cords.

WRAPPED HANGING LOOP

center ➞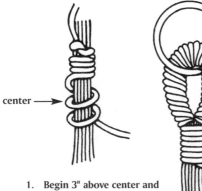

1. Begin 3" above center and wrap around all cords for 6".

2. Center the loop through ring and tie a gathering wrap around all cords.

WRAPPING A RING

BUTTERFLY or BUNDLE CORDS

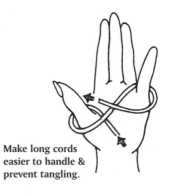

Make long cords easier to handle & prevent tangling.

rubber band

GATHERING WRAP

1. Make a long loop with the wrap cord and begin wrapping.

2. Continue wrapping and thread end of wrap cord through bottom loop.

3. Pull top cord to bury loop inside wrap.

4. Trim top wrap cord close to the wrap.

REVERSE LARK'S HEAD PLUS A HALF HITCH WITH EACH CORD

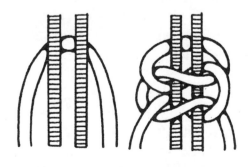

**ADDING A CORD
WITH A RIGHT-HAND
SQUARE KNOT.**

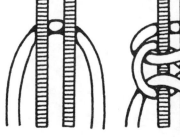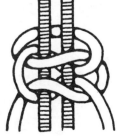

**ADDING A CORD
WITH A LEFT-HAND
SQUARE KNOT.**

LEFT HAND VERTICAL LARK'S HEAD SINNET

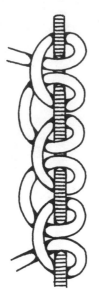

RIGHT HAND VERTICAL LARK'S HEAD SINNET

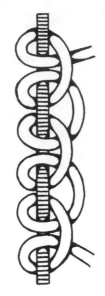

ALTERNATING VERTICAL LARK'S HEAD SINNET

Selecting Cords

Natural Jute Cord
This is a widely used cord in macramé. The thickness of the cord is determined by a numbering system. For example, in 4-ply #72 jute, the number 4 indicates how many plies are in each cord. The number 72 indicates the number of individual strands in each ply. Jute is a natural fiber so it will eventually rot if left outdoors in direct sunlight or wet weather over a long period of time. Therefore, jute is best for indoor or covered patio and screened porch use.

Polypropylene Cord
This cord is ideal for indoor and outdoor use. It is a synthetic cord that will often resist rot and is mildew proof. Although polypropylene fibers are formulated with added UV stabilizers for outdoor use, be aware that prolonged exposure to heat and sunlight can cause some deterioration in fiber strength. Polypropylene cords are available in various sizes and a wide variety of colors which are mostly colorfast and washable.

Waxed Cotton Jewelry Cord
This cord is ideal for jewelry projects because it is waxed and will hold the knots in place with no need for glue to secure cord ends. It is easy to knot and holds its shape effectively.

Helpful Hints

- Practice knot tying before beginning a project so that you can begin with confidence.

- It DOES NOT matter whether you tie right-hand square knots or left-hand square knots. Just be consistent throughout the pattern, unless otherwise directed.

- It is usually easier to work on a macramé project if it is suspended from a ceiling hook or an over-the-door hanger. Vary the height of the hanger by using scrap cord to hang your macramé at any height you need.

- When working with extremely long cords, bundle the cords by winding them around your hand and secure the center with a rubber band for easier knotting. You can tie much faster and release the cords as you need them.

- When cutting cords, you will be more accurate with cords lengths if you measure and cut one cord at a time. However, it is easier to measure the first cord and then use that one to measure and cut remaining cords.

- Splicing can be helpful if cords should break or they are too short to finish the project. To splice jute cord ends together, unravel cord ends and coat with white glue or hot glue, then twist them together. Wait for glue to dry before you continue knotting. Hot glue allows you to immediately resume knotting. To splice polypropylene cords, fuse or hot glue.

- Use an overhand knot on cord ends to prevent unraveling while knotting.

- When substituting cords in a pattern, try to use cords of equal thickness. If you change the diameter of the cords specified in the pattern, you will have to adjust the yardage for the pattern to work.

- When tying a half-knot-twist sinnet, let the sinnet twist as you tie it. Do not try to keep it flat. Always use the same side knotting cord for each knot. Keep the half knots horizontal so the twist is uniform and even.

- Keep the tension even when tying each and every knot. Keep the knots horizontal and the filler cords vertically straight. Keep rows of double half hitches straight and taut.

- It is easier to thread beads onto cord ends if you first tape or hot glue jute cord ends or fuse polypropylene cord ends to prevent unraveling.

- If you want to design your own hanger, allow four times the desired finished length DOUBLED. If you want long half-knot-twist sinnets, allow six times the desired finished length DOUBLED. Remember, the cords are centered through a ring, which is why they must be doubled.

Basic Belt

Pictured on Page 2

SUPPLIES

3-Ply #28 Natural Jute Cord - 60 yards
Thick Silver Metal Ring - 2" inside diameter
*If you can't find this metal ring at your local craft store,
look for it at home improvement or hardware stores.*

INSTRUCTIONS

Measure around your waist or hips, depending upon where you want the belt to rest. Then add a minimum of 10" for looping and knotting through the ring to determine your desired finished length.

1. CUT: 6 cords - 10 yards long

2. Fold all cords in half and lark's head each cord side-by-side onto the ring.

3. Pin cords to the knotting board and tie a row of 3 square knots close to the ring, using 4 cords for each square knot.

4. Alternate cords and tie a row of 2 square knots. *(The 2 outermost cords on each side are not used in knots on this row.)*

5. Continue to tie rows of alternating square knots *(3 per row, then 2 per row)* until you are 2" from your desired finished length, ending with a row of 2 square knots.

6. Tie a single square knot with the 4 center cords forming a V-shaped edge of alternating square knots.

7. Number cords 1-12 from the left to the right. Tie 3 V-shaped rows of double half hitches to finish the end of the belt:

    (a) Use cord 1 as the right diagonal anchor cord to the center & double half hitch cords 2-6 onto it.

    (b) Renumber cords. Use cord 12 as the left diagonal anchor cord to the center & double half hitch cords 11-6 onto it in this reverse order, creating a V-shaped edge of double half hitches.

    (c) Repeat steps (a) and (b) two times for 2 more rows of V-shaped double half hitches.

8. Trim cords close to the last row of double half hitches. Glue all knots to secure. Hot glue will give you a smooth edge if you mold the hot glue along the edge of the belt by wetting your fingers first before touching the hot glue to prevent getting burned.

Ridges Belt with optional fringe

Pictured on Front Cover

SUPPLIES

3.5mm - 4mm Braided Polypropylene Cord - 48 yards

Thick Silver Metal Ring - 2" inside diameter

If you can't find this metal ring at your local craft store, look for it at home improvement or hardware stores.

8mm Round Wood Beads or 6mm x 9mm Pony Beads - 8 for fringe

INSTRUCTIONS

Measure around your waist or hips, depending upon where you want the belt to rest. Then add a minimum of 8" for looping and knotting through the ring to determine your desired finished length.

1. CUT: 3 cords - 16 yards long

2. Fold each cord in half and mount them side-by-side onto the ring with a reverse lark's head plus a half hitch with each cord.

3. Use a rubber band to bundle cords for easier knotting.

4. Number cords 1-6 from left to right. Use cord 1 as the right horizontal anchor cord and double half hitch cords 2-6 onto it.

5. Renumber cords. Use cord 6 as the left horizontal anchor cord and double half hitch cords 5-1 onto it in this reverse order.

6. Continue to repeat steps 4 & 5 to desired finished length, always using the same anchor cord back and forth for the double half hitches.

7. Choose one of the following 2 methods for ending the belt:

   With Fringe - Cut cord ends to fringe length of your choice. Thread a bead onto each cord and tie an overhand knot at the end of the cord to hold the bead in place. Trim cord ends close to knots and fuse or glue to secure.

   Without Fringe - Trim cords close to the last row of double half hitches. Fuse the polypropylene cord ends into the row of double half hitches.

Note: When putting the belt on, pass the end of the belt through the metal ring from front to back so ridge design is showing.

White Diamonds Belt

Pictured on Page 2

SUPPLIES

3.5mm - 4mm White Braided Polypropylene Cord - 74 yards
6mm x 9mm White Pony Beads - 36

INSTRUCTIONS

Measure around your waist or upper hips, depending on where you want the belt to rest, to determine the desired finished length of the knotted section of the belt.

1. CUT: 12 cords - 6 yards long

2. Measure 36" from one end of each cord and pin the cords side-by-side to the knotting board at this point. Bundle long cords for easier knotting.

3. Tie a row of 3 square knots up close to the pins; using 2 knotting cords around 2 filler cords for each square knot. Alternate cords and tie a second row of 2 square knots *(the 2 outermost cords on each side are not used in knots on this row).* Tie a square knot with the 4 center cords in row 3.

4. Number cords 1-12 from the left to the right:

   (a) Use cord 1 as the right diagonal anchor cord to the center and double half hitch cords 2-6 onto it. Renumber cords

   (b) Use cord 12 as the left diagonal anchor cord to the center and double half hitch cords 11-6 onto it in this reverse order; this will connect the 2 diagonals and complete the V-shaped pattern of double half hitches.

   (c) Repeat steps (a) and (b) 2 more times for a total of 3 rows of V-shaped double half hitches.

5. Renumber cords. Tie a square knot with cords 1-5 using 2 knotting cords around 3 center filler cords. Repeat for cords 8-12.

6. Renumber cords 1-12 from the left to the right:

   (a) Use cord 6 as the left diagonal anchor cord to the outside edge and double half hitch cords 5-1 onto it in this reverse order.

   (b) Use cord 7 as the right diagonal anchor cord to the outside edge and double half hitch cords 8-12 onto it.

   (c) Renumber cords. Use cord 7 as the left diagonal anchor cord to the outside edge and double half hitch cords 6-1 onto it in this reverse order.

   (d) Renumber cords. Use cord 7 as the right diagonal anchor cord to the outside edge and double half hitch cords 8-12 onto it.

   (e) Renumber cords. Repeat steps (c) and (d) for a third row of inverted V-shaped double half hitches.

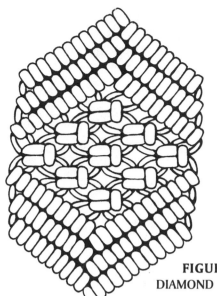

7. Renumber cords. Tie a 5-row diamond pattern of alternating square knots. (See FIGURE 1)

   (a) Begin with a single square knot using the 4 center cords (5-8) in the first row.

   (b) Alternate cords and tie 2 square knots in row 2.

   (c) Tie 3 alternating square knots in row 3 using all cords.

   (d) Tie 2 alternating square knots in row 4.

   (e) End with a single square knot in row 5 using the 4 center cords.

FIGURE 1
DIAMOND PATTERN

8. Continue to repeat steps 4 through 7 until you are approximately 2" short of your desired finished length, ending with step 4 *(three rows of V-shaped double half hitches)*.

9. Turn belt around to work on the other end *(where you made the first row of 3 square knots)*:

   (a) Tie a row of 2 alternating square knots. *(Note that you will be tying your square knots in the reverse direction from before. If you started the belt with right-hand square knots, then you will tie left-hand square knots to finish this end so that all knots in the belt will look the same.)*

   (b) Then tie a square knot with the 4 center cords, completing a diamond pattern of alternating square knots at this end of the belt.

10. Repeat step 4 to finish this end of the belt with 3 rows of V-shaped double half hitches.

11. Renumber cords. Tie an accumulated edge of double half hitches from the left side to the center using cords 1-6. (See FIGURE 2)

   (a) Use cord 1 as the right diagonal anchor cord to the center and double half hitch cord 2 onto it.

   (b) Use cords 1 and 2 together as the anchor cord and double half hitch cord 3 onto both of them.

   (c) Use cords 1-3 together as the anchor cords and double half hitch cord 4 onto all 3 of them.

   (d) Use cords 1-4 together as the anchor cords and double half hitch cord 5 onto all 4 of them.

   (e) Use cords 1-5 together as the anchor cords and double half hitch cord 6 onto all 5 of them.

FIGURE 2
ACCUMULATED EDGE OF
DOUBLE HALF HITCHES

INSTRUCTIONS CONTINUED ON PAGE 14

12. Renumber cords and tie an accumulated edge of double half hitches from the right side to the center using cords 12-7 in this reverse order (see FIGURE 3).

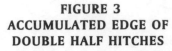

FIGURE 3
ACCUMULATED EDGE OF
DOUBLE HALF HITCHES

(a) Use cord 12 as the left diagonal anchor cord to the center and double half hitch cord 11 onto it.

(b) Use cords 12 and 11 together as the anchor cords and double half hitch cord 10 onto both of them.

(c) Use cords 12-10 together as the anchor cords and double half hitch cord 9 onto all 3 of them.

(d) Use cords 12-9 together as the anchor cords and double half hitch cord 8 onto all 4 of them.

(e) Use cords 12-8 together as the anchor cords and double half hitch cord 7 onto all 5 of them.

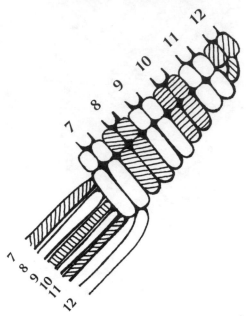

13. Cut a wrapping cord 1 yard long. Gather all cords together from each accumulated edge in the center where they meet and wrap for ½". Trim both wrapping cord ends close to the wrap. Also, trim 6 of the cords coming out of the wrap, leaving 6 remaining cords. Fuse or glue polypropylene cords into the wrap.

14. Repeat steps 11-13 on the other end of the belt.

15. Trim all remaining cords to 18" or desired finished length. Thread 3 pony beads onto each cord end and tie in place with an overhand knot. Trim knot and fuse or glue to secure.

Fancy Flip-Flops

Pictured on Front Cover

SUPPLIES
Vinyl Flip-Flops - 1 Pair in size of your choice
3.5mm - 4mm Braided Polypropylene Cord - 14 yards
   (or 2mm Pepperell SU-PREME Natural Waxed Cotton Jewelry
   Cord - 20 yards)

INSTRUCTIONS

1. Cut: 2 Polypropylene knotting cords - 7 yards long
      or 2 Natural waxed cotton knotting cords - 10 yards long

2. Working on one flip-flop, fold one cord in half and add it to the strap *(which becomes the filler)* with a square knot at the heel end of the flip-flop. Push the knot up close to the sole of the flip- flop.

3. Continue to tie a sinnet of square knots using 2 knotting cords around the vinyl strap filler. Keep pushing each knot up close to the previous knot so that the strap is tightly covered.

4. When you reach the center toe strap, continue tying tight knots to prevent any big gaps along the strap as you pass over the toe strap onto the next side.

5. Continue knotting the other side of the strap until you reach the end, pushing all knots up close to each other.

6. **If using polypropylene cord**, trim both cord ends close to the last square knot and fuse to secure.

   If using cotton cord, tie an overhand knot in each cord end close to the last square knot, and trim.

7. Repeat steps 2 through 6 for the second flip-flop.

Sling Purse *in length desired*

Pictured on Page 2

FIGURE 1

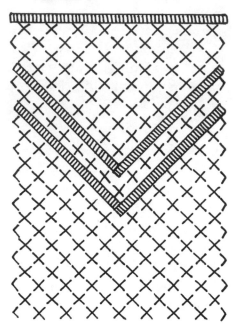

Size of Finished Purse:
6 ½" wide x 7 ½ - 9" long + strap length as desired

SUPPLIES

3.5mm - 4mm Braided Polypropylene Cord - 100 yards
Optional: ¾"-1" wide Velcro strip - 6" long

INSTRUCTIONS

1. CUT: 1 holding cord - 4 yards long
    32 knotting cords - 2 ½ yards long
    1 strap knotting cord - 16 yards long

2. Find the center of the 4-yard holding cord and pin it to the knotting board. Then pin the holding cord horizontally to the board to the right and left of the center pin.

3. Fold one knotting cord in half and mount it onto the holding cord to the left of the center pin with a reverse lark's head plus a half hitch with each cord. Repeat for mounting 15 more knotting cords side-by-side to the left side of the center pin.

4. Fold the remaining 16 knotting cords in half and mount them side-by-side onto the right side of the holding cord using a reverse lark's head plus a half hitch with each cord. There are now 32 cords mounted onto the holding cord.

5. Tie a row of 16 square knots up close to the holding cord using 2 knotting cords around 2 filler cords for each square knot.

6. Tie a row of alternating square knots in the second row.

7. Unpin the cords from the knotting board and fold in half. Tie the 2 holding cord ends together with a shoestring knot at one end of the purse. These 2 holding cords will not be used again until they become filler cords for the strap in step 21.

8. Tie an alternating square knot with the 4 loose cords in row 2 at the end of the purse, connecting the front and backside of the purse. Repin cords to knotting board to continue working.

9. *Working on the front side of the purse only:* Tie a third row of 8 alternating square knots. Then tie a fourth row of 7 alternating square knots centered beneath the 3rd row. Continue to tie 6 more decreasing rows of alternating square knots until you have 1 center square knot in row 10. (See FIGURE 1)

10. Number the cords on this front side 1-32 from the left to the right.

    (a) Use cord 1 as the right diagonal anchor cord to the center and double half hitch cords 2-16 onto it. Renumber cords.

    (b) Use cord 32 as the left diagonal anchor cord to the center and double half hitch cords 31-16 onto it, in this reverse order, creating a V-shaped pattern of double half hitches. Unpin purse.

11. Turn purse over to backside and repin to knotting board. Repeat steps 9 & 10.

12. Unpin purse. *Working on one END of the purse:* Tie a square knot using 2 cords from the last row on the back of the purse plus 2 cords from the same row on the front of the purse. Repeat for tying a square knot on the other END of the purse.

13. Repin front side of the purse to the knotting board. *Working on the front side of the purse:* Beginning on the left, tie an alternating square knot using 2 cords from the END square knot and 2 cords from the double half hitches. Continue to tie a right diagonal row of alternating square knots to the center. (See FIGURE 1)

    Repeat for a left diagonal row of alternating square knots to the center. Tie a square knot with the 4 center cords at the point of the "V", creating a V-shaped row of alternating square knots. Turn purse over to backside, repin to board and repeat to tie a V-shaped row of alternating square knots on the back.

14. Renumber cords and repeat step 10 for another row of V-shaped double half hitches on the back.

15. Unpin the purse, turn over and repin purse to the knotting board so that you are ready to work on the front of the purse. Renumber cords and repeat step 10 for a second row of double half hitches on the front.

16. Unpin the purse from the knotting board. Flatten the purse on one end and repin to the board so that you can work with the loose cords on this end.

17. To fill in the end section and connect the front and back of the purse, tie a square knot in the point of the inverted "V" pattern of double half hitches using 2 cords from the front row of double half hitches and 2 cords from the back row of double half hitches.

18. *Continue to fill in the end section of the purse:* Tie 7 more rows of increasing alternating square knots, picking up 2 new cords at each end of each new row from the double half hitches.

19. Repeat steps 16-18 to fill in the section at the other end of the purse with increasing alternating square knots.

INSTRUCTIONS CONTINUED ON PAGE 18

20. Continue to tie 7, 9 or 11 more rows of alternating square knots *(depending on how long you want the purse to be)* ALL THE WAY AROUND THE PURSE.

21. To close the bottom of the purse:
   (a) Turn purse inside out.

   (b) Flatten purse so that the front and back are lined up evenly with a row of 8 square knots on the front and the back, with the 2 loose strap cords positioned at one end.

   (c) Turn purse upside down and place it between your knees.

   (d) Begin knotting at the farthest end of the purse. Tie a tight square knot with no filler cords (see FIGURE 2) using only the first 2 cords at the end of the purse *(one cord from the front side and the corresponding cord from the back side - see FIGURE 3, Step 1).*

FIGURE 2
Square Knot with
no filler cords

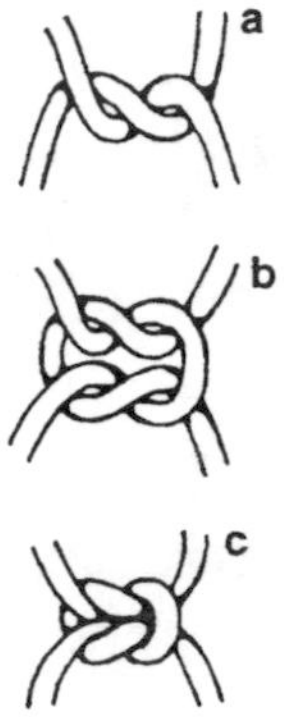

FIGURE 3
Close Bottom of Pouch
Square knots in diagram represent bottom row of square knots on purse

Step 1
1st Square Knot
with no filler cords.
2 dotted knotting cords
(1 end cord from opposite sides)

Step 2
2nd Square Knot
1 black filler cord and
1 striped knotting cord from
opposite sides

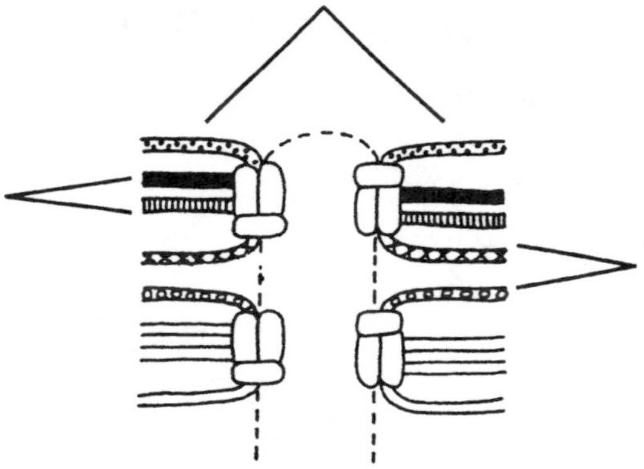

Step 3
3rd Square Knot
1 "xxxxx" filler cord and
1 "ooooo" knotting cord
from opposite sides

Step 4
Continue to close bottom with 4-cord
square knots leaving 2 loose cords at the
end. Tie a square knot with no filler
cords with these last 2 cords.

   (e) Tie the next tight square knot using the next 2 cords from the front side plus the next 2 corresponding cords from the backside of the purse. Use 1 cord from each side as a knotting cord and the other cord from each side as a filler cord (see FIGURE 3 - Step 2). Flip these cords from the completed square knot up out of the way to continue knotting.

   (f) Continue tying these 4-cord square knots tightly along the bottom of the purse. There will be 2 cords left at the end of the row. (See FIGURE 3 - Steps 3 & 4)

   (g) Tie a square knot with no filler cords with these last 2 cords as you did in step (d) to finish closing the bottom of the purse. (See FIGURE 2)

   (h) Pull each filler cord taut along the bottom so there is no slack in the cord.

(i) Working on one square knot at a time, cut each cord ¼" in length. Fuse each cord into the square knot to secure.

(j) Turn purse back right-side-out so that the fused knots are on the inside of the purse.

22. *The following directions are for the strap:* There is enough yardage to tie a strap that criss-crosses the body from the shoulder with the purse resting on the hip. Of course, the length of the strap is optional to fit your preference.

(a) The 2 loose cords at the end of the purse become the filler cords for the strap square knot sinnet.

(b) Fold the long 16-yard knotting cord in half and lark's head it onto the horizontal holding cord next to the shoestring knot at the END of the purse with the filler cords. Bundle these long cords for easier knotting.

(c) Use the 2 long knotting cords to tie a sinnet of square knots around the 2 short filler cords. Continue until you have the length of strap desired.

23. To connect the strap to the other end of the purse:

(a) Thread all 4 strap cords through the opening at the other end of the purse, threading the cords from the outside towards the inside of the purse.

(b) Fold these 4 cords back up against themselves crossing over the holding cord.

(c) Use 2 cords together as a knotting cord on each side and tie a multiple cord square knot around the doubled (back-to-back) filler cords to secure the strap to this end of the purse. This multiple cord square knot fits right next to the strap. You should not be able to see any filler cords when the strap is secured to the end of the purse. Pull each cord taut from this multiple cord square knot.

(d) Trim all 4 cords close to the multiple cord square knot and fuse to secure.

24. *Optional closure:* Cut a strip of Velcro to fit the inside of the purse along the top edge. Separate Velcro strips and secure inside the purse opening.

This-n-That Bracelet & Choker

Pictured on Front Cover

BRACELET SUPPLIES
2mm Pepperell SU-PREME Natural Waxed
   Cotton Jewelry Cord - 3 yards
6mm x 9mm Pony Beads - 6-9 beads

CHOKER SUPPLIES
2mm Pepperell SU-PREME Natural Waxed
   Cotton Jewelry Cord - 5 yards
6mm x 9mm Pony Beads - 12-16 beads

FIGURE 1
JEWELRY FASTENING LOOP
Add a cord with a square knot
to a folded filler cord to create
a fastening loop.

INSTRUCTIONS

1. CUT:
   For Bracelet - 1 knotting cord - 2 yards long
                1 filler cord - 30" long

   For Choker - 1 knotting cord - 3 ½ yards long
                1 filler cord - 1 ½ yards long

FIGURE 2

2. Fold the short filler cord in half and pin the center of the cord to the knotting board. Fold the long knotting cord in half and add it to the 2 filler cords with a square knot ⅝" from the pin, leaving a fastening loop. (See FIGURE 1)

3. Tie 2 more square knots.

4. Thread a bead onto the 2 center filler cords and tie a half-knot-twist sinnet under the bead containing 6 half knots. (See FIGURE 2)

5. Thread a bead onto the 2 filler cords and tie 3 square knots under the bead.

6. Continue this pattern (steps 4 & 5), alternating beads with a half-knot-twist sinnet and 3 square knots, until the piece is long enough to fit around your wrist or neck.

7. At the end of the sinnet, leave a ¼" space after the last knot and tie a multiple cord overhand knot with all 4 cords together. The fastening loop will rest in this space when the jewelry is worn. Pull each cord taut out of the overhand knot. Trim all 4 cords close to the overhand knot.

The overhand knot may initially fit tightly through the fastening loop, but the loop will stretch with wear. If the loop is too tight, slide a pencil through the loop and stretch it a bit.

Free Spirit Bracelet & Choker

Pictured on Page 2

> **BRACELET SUPPLIES**
> 2mm Pepperell SU-PREME Natural Waxed
> Cotton Jewelry Cord - 4 yards
>
> **CHOKER SUPPLIES**
> 2mm Pepperell SU-PREME Natural Waxed
> Cotton Jewelry Cord - 6 ½ yards

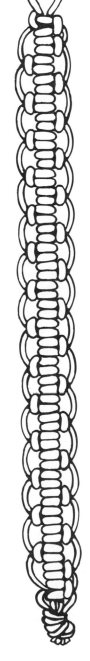

FIGURE 1
JEWELRY FASTENING LOOP
Add a cord with a square knot
to a folded filler cord to create
a fastening loop.

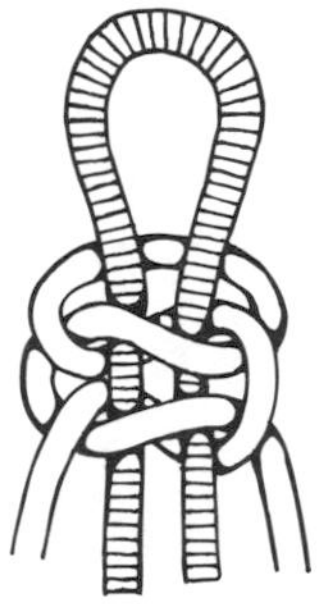

FIGURE 2

INSTRUCTIONS

1. CUT:
For Bracelet - 1 knotting cord - 3 yards long
                 1 filler cord - 30" long

For Choker - 1 knotting cord - 5 yards long
                1 filler cord - 1 ½ yards long

2. Fold the short filler cord in half and pin the center to the knotting board. Fold the long knotting cord in half and add it to the 2 filler cords with a square knot ⅝" from the pin, leaving a fastening loop. (See FIGURE 1)

3. Tie a right-hand vertical lark's head knot around the 2 center filler cords using the long knotting cord on the right side. *(Note that you will get a different finished look depending upon whether you form larger loops or smaller loops when tying the vertical lark's head knots.)*

4. Tie a left-hand vertical lark's head knot around the 2 center filler cords using the long knotting cord on the left.

5. Continue to tie a sinnet of alternating lark's head knots (See FIGURE 2) long enough to fit around your wrist or neck.

6. At the end of the sinnet, leave a ¼" space after the last knot and tie a multiple cord overhand knot with all 4 cords together. The fastening loop will rest in this ¼" space when jewelry is worn. Pull each cord taut out of the overhand knot. Trim all 4 cords close to the overhand knot.

The overhand knot may initially fit tightly through the fastening loop, but the loop will stretch with wear. If the loop is too tight, slide a pencil through the loop and stretch it a bit.

Simple Key Ring

Pictured on Page 2

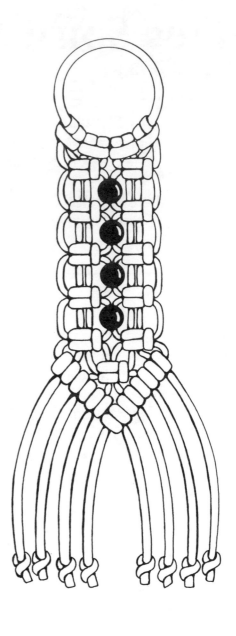

Finished Length: 7" to 8"

SUPPLIES

2mm Pepperell SU-PREME Natural Waxed
   Cotton Jewelry Cord - 4 yards
10mm Natural Wood Beads - 4
1 ¼" Silver Split Key Ring - 1

INSTRUCTIONS

1. CUT: 4 cords - 1 yard long

2. Fold all 4 cords in half and lark's head each cord side-by-side onto the split key ring.

3. Tie a square knot with each group of 4 cords up next to the ring.

4. Thread the 2 center cords through a bead. Tie a row of 2 square knots under the bead to hold it in place.

5. Repeat step 4 three more times to add 3 more beads.

6. Tie an alternating square knot with the 4 center cords.

7. Number cords 1 through 8 from the left to the right:

   (a) Use cord 1 as the right diagonal anchor cord to the center and double half hitch cords 2-4 onto it.

   (b) Renumber cords. Use cord 8 as the left diagonal anchor cord to the center and double half hitch cords 7-4 onto it, in this reverse order, creating a V-shaped row of double half hitches.

8. Trim cord ends to 4". Tie an overhand knot in each cord end. Waxed cotton cord does not need glue to hold the knots. DO NOT FUSE WAXED COTTON CORD. If using jute or hemp cord, glue the knots to secure. Fuse polypropylene cord ends.

Sounds of Summer Bell Chime

Pictured on Page 51

Finished Length: 25"

SUPPLIES

6mm Braided Polypropylene Cord - 25 ⅓ yards - Pearl (COLOR A)
                                                        24 yards - Sage (COLOR B)

4" Metal Ring - 1
Terra Cotta Pot - 4 ½" high x 4 ½" wide
16mm Natural Wood Beads - 4
20mm Wood Bead - 1
Natural Sea Sponge - for texturizing rim of pot
Chunky Stamp - for decorating pot
Paint Brush
DecoArt Patio Paint -
  Antique Mum (COLOR A)
  Sprout Green (COLOR B)
(Select colors that match or coordinate with the colors of your cords)

INSTRUCTIONS

1. Paint clay pot and let dry.

   Sample was painted with Antique Mum base coat (COLOR A) to match Pearl cord and sponge painted with Sprout Green (COLOR B) around the rim. The ivy stamp design was also applied with Sprout Green paint.

2. Cut: 1 COLOR A Wrapping Cord - 1 ⅓ yards long

   Tie one end of the cord onto the metal ring. Tightly wrap the entire ring. Untie the first knot, trim both cord ends and fuse both cords together on the ring.

3. Cut: 4 COLOR A cords - 6 yards long
        4 COLOR B cords - 6 yards long

   (a) Fold the COLOR A cords in half and lark's head each cord side-by-side onto the ring, over the section on the ring where the cords were joined together.

   (b) Fold the COLOR B cords in half and lark's head each cord side-by-side onto the ring to the right of the COLOR A cords. Bundle COLOR B cords with a rubber band and lay them up over the macramé board to get them out of the way.

4. COLOR A CORDS ONLY: Number the 8 cords on the left 1 through 8 from the left to the right.

   (a) Tie 8 rows of angling double half hitches to the right as follows: Use cord 1 as the right horizontal holding cord and double half hitch cords 2 through 8 onto it. Renumber cords EACH time and repeat for 7 more rows of angling double half hitches to the right. (See FIGURE 1 on page 24)

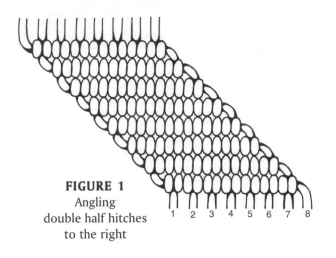

FIGURE 1
Angling
double half hitches
to the right

1 2 3 4 5 6 7 8

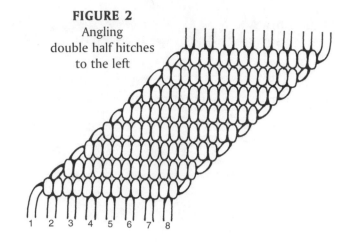

FIGURE 2
Angling
double half hitches
to the left

1 2 3 4 5 6 7 8

(b) Renumber cords. Tie 8 rows of angling double half hitches to the left as follows: Beginning with cord 8 as the left horizontal holding cord, double half hitch cords 7 through 1 onto it, in this reverse order. Renumber cords EACH time and repeat for 7 more rows of angling double half hitches to the left. (See FIGURE 2)

(c) Renumber cords and repeat step (a) to create a zig-zag pattern of angling double half hitches.

5. Renumber the 8 COLOR A cords and continue to renumber the cords as you tie each row. Tie 8 rows of decreasing double half hitches as follows:

(a) Use cord 8 as the left horizontal holding cord and double half hitch cords 7-1 onto it in this reverse order.

(b) Renumber cords again and use cord 8 as the left horizontal holding cord and double half hitch cords 7-2 onto it, in this reverse order. DO NOT DOUBLE HALF HITCH THE PREVIOUS HOLDING CORD FROM THE FIRST ROW.

(c) Continue to tie 6 more rows of decreasing double half hitches, dropping the previous holding cord per row, until you double half hitch cord 7 onto cord 8 in row 8. (See FIGURE 3)

1 2 3 4 5 6 7 8

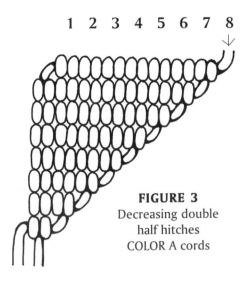

FIGURE 3
Decreasing double
half hitches
COLOR A cords

1 2 3 4 5 6 7 8

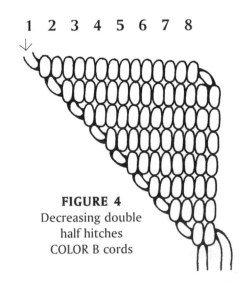

FIGURE 4
Decreasing double
half hitches
COLOR B cords

(d) Flip the completed COLOR A zig-zag pattern of angling double half hitches up out of the way to continue knotting with COLOR B cords.

6. COLOR B CORDS ONLY: Number the 8 cords on the right 1 through 8 from the left to the right. Tie 8 rows of angling double half hitches to the left as follows:

(a) Use cord 8 as the left horizontal holding cord and double half hitch cords 7 through 1 onto it in this reverse order. Renumber cords EACH time and repeat for 7 more rows of angling double half hitches to the left. (See FIGURE 2)

(b) Renumber cords. Tie 8 rows of angling double half hitches to the right as follows: Beginning with cord 1 as the right horizontal holding cord, double half hitch cords 2-8 onto it. Renumber cords EACH time and repeat for 7 more rows of angling double half hitches to the right. (See FIGURE 1)

(c) Renumber cords and repeat step (a) to create a zig-zag pattern of angling double half hitches.

7. Renumber the 8 COLOR B cords and continue to renumber the cords as you tie each row. Tie 8 rows of decreasing double half hitches as follows:

(a) Use cord 1 as the right horizontal holding cord and double half hitch cords 2-8 onto it.

(b) Renumber cords again and use cord 1 as the right horizontal holding cord and double half hitch cords 2-7 onto it. DO NOT DOUBLE HALF HITCH THE PREVIOUS HOLDING CORD FROM THE FIRST ROW.

(c) Continue to tie 6 more rows of decreasing double half hitches, dropping the previous holding cord per row, until you double half hitch cord 2 onto cord 1 in row 8. (See FIGURE 4)

8. When both sections are the same length, interlock them following the diagram in FIGURE 5.

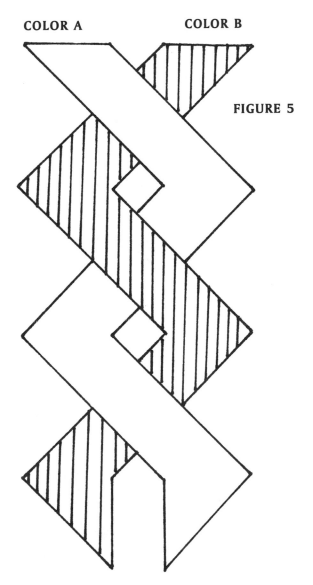

COLOR A   COLOR B

FIGURE 5

INSTRUCTIONS CONTINUED ON PAGE 26

9. Tie a center square knot with the bottom 4 cords *(2 COLOR B cords from the last row of double half hitches on the left and 2 COLOR A cords from the last row of double half hitches on the right.)* The remaining knotting cords are pulled to the BACK SIDE so that the 2 zig-zag sections of double half hitches meet flush in the center.

10. Turn project over so that you are working on the BACK SIDE:

    (a) Beginning at the top of the remaining loose cords, use a COLOR A cord plus a corresponding COLOR B cord and tie the 2 cords together tightly.

    (b) Repeat this until all 6 pairs of cords are connected, joining the 2 sections on the back side.

    (c) Trim these 6 pairs of cords close to the knots and fuse to secure. DO NOT CUT OFF THE 4 CORDS FROM THE CENTER SQUARE KNOT. Turn project over to the front side to add the clay pot bell.

11. TO ADD THE CLAY POT BELL: Thread all 4 cords through the hole in the clay pot. Then thread all 4 cords through the larger bead. Tie a multiple cord overhand knot with all 4 cords together next to the bead, pushing it up against the inside of the pot.

12. Thread a small bead onto each cord end and tie an overhand knot to hold the bead in place, hanging at varying lengths 4"-6" below the small hole in the pot. Trim each cord close to the knot and fuse to secure.

Twist & Turn Hanger

Pictured on Back Cover

Finished length with tail cords: 5' 4"

Supplies
4-ply #72 Natural Jute Cord - 69 yards
  (or 6mm Braided Polypropylene Cord)
Large Wood Beads (20mm to 38mm - your choice) - 20
1 ½" or 2" Soldered Metal Ring - 1

INSTRUCTIONS

1. CUT: 4 Long Knotting Cords - 11 yards long
        4 Short Filler Cords - 5 yards long
        1 Wrapping Cord - 2 yards long

2. Center all 8 cords through the metal ring. Gather all 16 cords together and tie a 3" gathering wrap close to the ring with the 2-yard cord. Pull each cord taut against the ring. Trim both of these short cords close to the wrap and fuse or glue to secure.

3. Divide cords into 4 groups of 4 cords each with 2 long and 2 short cords in each group.

4. Working with one group of 4 cords, tie a half-knot-twist sinnet that is 8" long using 2 long knotting cords around 2 short filler cords. Be sure to push the first knot up close to the wrap.

5. Thread a bead onto the 2 center filler cords and tie 12 half knots under the bead. Repeat this step four more times to add a total of 5 beads to the sinnet.

6   Continue tying the half-knot-twist sinnet under the last bead for 8 inches, ending with a square knot.

7. Repeat steps 4 through 6 for the remaining three groups of cords to complete the 4 plant hanger sinnets.

8. To connect the sinnets and form the cradle:
    (a) Drop down 5" from the end of the half-knot-twist sinnets and tie a row of alternating square knots.

    (b) Drop down 2" from the last row of square knots and tie a row of alternating square knots.

    (c) Close the bottom of the cradle by tying a row of alternating square knots next to the last row of knots.

9. Cut a wrapping cord 3 yards long. Gather all cords together under the cradle and tie a 2" gathering wrap. Trim only the top wrap cord close to the wrap, letting the bottom cord hang with the tail cords. Trim tail cords to 12" or desired length. Fuse or glue cord ends to prevent unraveling.

Starlite-Jarlite

Pictured on Back Cover

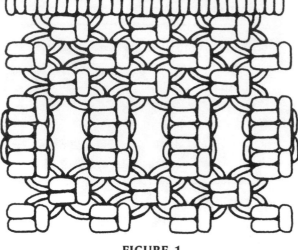

FIGURE 1

INSTRUCTIONS

1. Because the diameters of the polypropylene and jute cords vary, you will need to cut more jute cords for this project than polypropylene cords. Always remember to add cords in multiples of 2 to the holding cord when adjusting the number of cords to go around the jar.

    CUT: 1 holding cord - ⅔ yard long
    20 Polypropylene knotting cords - 1 ⅔ yards long
    OR
    24 Natural Jute knotting cords - 2 yards long

2. Pin the holding cord horizontally to the knotting board.

3. Fold each knotting cord in half and mount it onto the holding cord with a reverse lark's head knot plus a half hitch with each cord.

4. Tie a row of square knots up close to the lark's head knots, using 2 knotting cords around 2 filler cords for each square knot.

5. Remove the cords from the knotting board and tightly tie the 2 holding cords ends together with a double shoestring knot around the ribbed neck of the jar. Trim both cord ends close to the knot and fuse or hot glue the knot to secure.

6. Tie 2 rows of alternating square knots all the way around the jar, connecting all cords.

7. Alternate cords and tie a square knot sinnet with each group of 4 cords. Select appropriate instructions for cord used:

    (a) **Polypropylene cord:** Tie a sinnet of 3 square knots with each group of cords. (See FIGURE 1)

    (b) **Jute cord:** Tie a sinnet of 4 square knots with each group of cords.

8. Continue to tie 10-12 more rows of alternating square knots around the jar until you reach the bottom. The number of rows may vary depending on how tightly or loosely you tie your knots and upon the diameter of the cord used. It will take more rows of jute cord to reach the bottom than polypropylene cord.

9. Hold the jar upside down between your legs for easier knotting. Continue tying 2 or 3 more rows of alternating square knots over the edge and onto the bottom of the jar, pulling each row of square knots tightly, up close to the previous row, to condense the area of cords. *(It may take 4 rows if using jute cord.)*

10. *(Read this entire step before cutting cords.)* To eliminate the number of cords on the bottom of the jar, TRIM ONLY EACH PAIR OF KNOTTING CORDS close to each square knot. This leaves only the filler cords from each square knot on the bottom of the jar. Choose the appropriate method for securing cords:

    (a) **Jute Cord:** When you eliminate jute cords on the bottom of the jar, you must hot glue the entire square knot to keep the knot from coming untied, as the cut cords have a tendency to slip loose. Glue the knot <u>first</u> and then cut the knotting cords.

    (b) **Polypropylene cord:** Fuse cut ends into the square knot to hold the cords in place.

11. Tie a square knot with each group of 4 cords around the bottom of the jar, using 2 filler cords from each of 2 adjacent square knots to make 4 cords for each new square knot.

12. To eliminate more cords on the bottom: Trim each KNOTTING CORD close to the square knot and fuse or glue to secure as before. This leaves only filler cords from the prior square knots on the bottom of the jar.

13. You now have 10 to 12 cords left on the bottom depending upon how many cords you started with.

    Choose one of the following 2 methods to finish the bottom:

    10 CORDS: Divide the remaining 10 cords into 2 groups of 5 cords each. Tie a tight square knot with each group of cords using 2 knotting cords around 3 center filler cords. Trim all 5 cords close to each square knot and fuse or glue to secure. Fuse or glue these 2 knots together to make a flat bottom.

    12 CORDS: Divide cords into 3 groups of 4 cords each. Tie 1 or 2 tight square knots with each group of 4 cords - the 3 groups of cords must touch together at this point. Trim all cords close to each square knot and fuse or hot glue to secure. Fuse or hot glue these 3 knots together to make a flat bottom.

14. Place the glass votive holder inside the mouth of the jar with the lip of the votive holder resting on the rim of the jar.

Wall Pouch

Ideal to hold a narrow vase or wooden spoons in your kitchen.

Pictured on Front Cover

Finished Length: 27"

SUPPLIES
6mm Braided Polypropylene Cord - 53 yards
(or 4-ply #72 Natural Jute Cord)

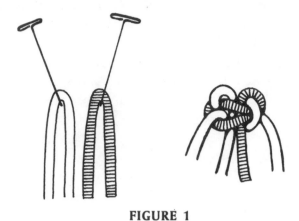

FIGURE 1

INSTRUCTIONS

1. CUT: 2 knotting cords - 4 yards long
   2 filler cords - 3 ½ yards long

2. Measure 1 ⅔ yards from the end of all 4 cords and pin them side-by-side to the knotting board, with the 2 long knotting cords on the outside of the 2 shorter center filler cords. Lay the top 1 ⅔ yards of the cords over the top of your knotting board so they are not in your way.

3. Tie a square knot next to the pins, using the 2 long knotting cords around the 2 shorter filler cords. Continue to tie 11 more square knots in this sinnet. Unpin and remove cords from the board.

4. Cut: 12 new cords - 3 yards long.
   Working with one pair of cords, fold the 2 cords in half and pin the centers side-by-side to the knotting board. Tie a square knot next to the pins to join the 4 cords into a square knot. (See FIGURE 1) Repeat for each of the 5 remaining pairs of cords.

5. Pin one of the new square knots to the board. Bend the square knot sinnet (completed in steps 2 & 3) into a flat arc and pin it to the board on either side of the new square knot. The last square knot on each end of the sinnet should line up in a row with the new square knot. (See FIGURE 2)

6. Pin 2 new square knots to the left side of the sinnet. Pin 3 new square knots to the right side of the sinnet. You now have a row of 8 square knots with 32 working cords across the board. (See FIGURE 2)

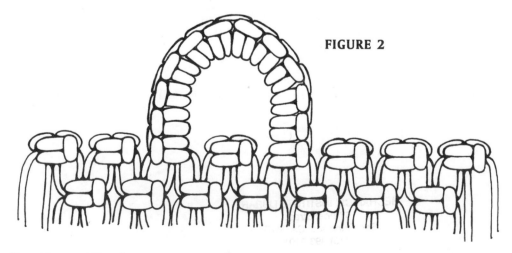

FIGURE 2

7. Tie a row of alternating square knots connecting all cords.

8. Unpin both groups of side knots. Bring the cords from each side forward to the front and tie an alternating square knot, using 2 cords from each side to connect the row of knots in the front and begin to form a tubular pouch.

9. Remove cords from the knotting board and hang on a doorknob for easier knotting. Tie a third row of alternating square knots all the way around the pouch. Tie a fourth row of square knots all around the pouch, <u>but do not alternate cords,</u> creating a row of 2-square-knot-sinnets around the pouch.

10. Continue to tie 11 more rows of alternating square knots all the way around the pouch.

11. Flatten pouch so that there are 4 square knots in the last row across the front and back of the pouch.

12. *Working on the front side only*: Tie a row of 3 alternating square knots. Then tie a row of 2 alternating square knots working only with the 8 center cords. Turn the pouch over and repeat these 2 rows on the back side.

13. Cut a wrapping cord 1 ½ yards long. Gather all cords together directly below the last row of square knots and tie a 1" gathering wrap. Trim the top wrap cord close to the wrap. Trim all tail cords to desired length. *(If there are any short tail cords, trim those cords close to the wrap so that all cords appear to be equal in length.)* Glue jute cord ends or fuse polypropylene cord ends to prevent unraveling.

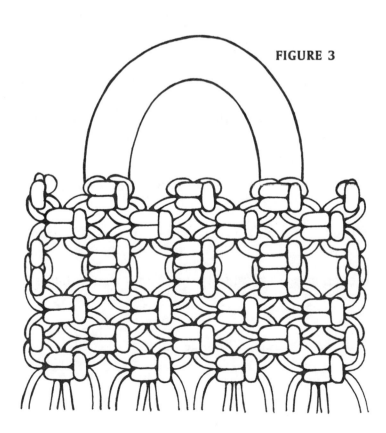

FIGURE 3

Chinese Crown Knot Hanger

Pictured on Back Cover

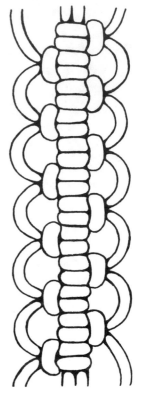

FIGURE 1

Finished Length: 4 ½ feet

SUPPLIES

6mm Braided Polypropylene Cord - 63 yards
  (or 4-Ply #72 Natural Jute Cord)
1 ½" or 2" Soldered Metal Ring - 1

INSTRUCTIONS

1. **Cut:** 4 knotting cords - 10 yards long
       4 filler cords - 5 yards long
       1 wrapping cord - 1 yard long

2. Place all 8 cords through the metal ring until cords are centered. Gather all 16 cords together and tie a 1" gathering wrap with the 1 yard cord. Trim both ends of the wrapping cord close to the wrap and fuse or glue ends to secure.

3. Divide the cords into 4 groups of 4 cords each, with 2 long knotting cords and 2 shorter filler cords in each group. Bundle each group of cords with a rubber band for easier knotting.

4. Place the ring and cords upside down between your knees for easier knotting. Tie a Chinese Crown Knot 6" long. Be sure to pull each cord taut as you tie each knot. You must position the cords so that they lay flat and do not twist as they come out of the previous crown knot.

5. Hang the ring from a ceiling hook or an over-the-door-hanger to tie the straps.

6. Working with 1 group of 4 cords, remove the rubber band and tie the first hanger strap using the 2 long knotting cords to tie a sinnet of alternating vertical lark's head knots around the 2 short filler cords as follows: (See FIGURE 1)

    (a) Tie a right-hand vertical lark's head knot using the long right-hand knotting cord around the 2 short filler cords.

    (b) Tie a left-hand vertical lark's head knot using the long left-hand knotting cord around the 2 short filler cords.

    (c) Continue to tie an alternating vertical lark's head knot sinnet that is 22" long.

    (d) End the sinnet with a square knot.

7. Repeat step 6 for each of the remaining 3 bundled groups of cords.

8. Connect all sinnets and form the cradle of the hanger as follows:

  (a) Drop down 6" and tie a row of alternating square knots.

  (b) Drop down 3" and tie a second row of alternating square knots.

  (c) Tie a third row of alternating square knots up close to the previous row of knots.

9. Cut a 2-yard wrapping cord. Gather all tail cords together and wrap for 2".   Trim the top wrap cord close to the wrap and fuse or glue cord end to secure. Let the bottom wrap cord hang with the tail cords. Trim all tail cords to 12" or desired finished length. Fuse polypropylene cord ends to prevent unraveling. Glue jute cord ends.

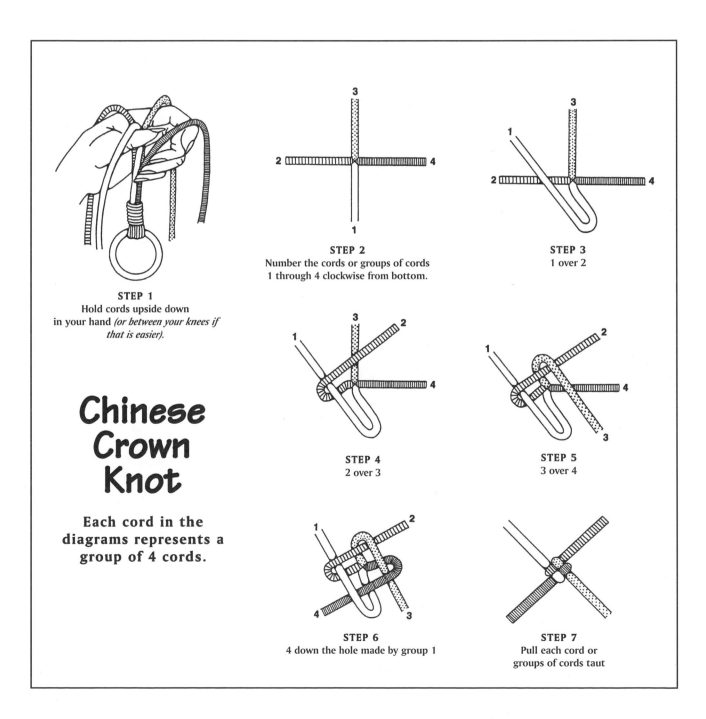

STEP 1
Hold cords upside down
in your hand *(or between your knees if
that is easier)*.

Chinese Crown Knot

Each cord in the diagrams represents a group of 4 cords.

STEP 2
Number the cords or groups of cords
1 through 4 clockwise from bottom.

STEP 3
1 over 2

STEP 4
2 over 3

STEP 5
3 over 4

STEP 6
4 down the hole made by group 1

STEP 7
Pull each cord or
groups of cords taut

Squared Away Hanger

Pictured on Page 51

Finished Length: 6 ½ feet

SUPPLIES

4-ply #72 Natural Jute Cord - 148 yards
  (or 6mm Braided Polypropylene Cord)
2 ½" Soldered Metal Ring - 1

INSTRUCTIONS

1. CUT:
   12 knotting cords - 12 yards long
   1 gathering wrap cord - 2 yards long

2. Center all cords through the metal ring. Gather all 24 cords together and tie a gathering wrap for 2" using the 2-yard cord. Pull each cord taut against the ring. Trim the 2 short cord ends close to the wrap and glue or fuse to secure.

3. Divide the long cords into 4 groups of 6 cords each. Bundle each group of cords with a rubber band. Place ring and cords upside down between your legs for easier knotting.

4. Tie a square lanyard knot, following the diagrams in FIGURE 1. Pull each individual cord in each 6-cord group taut as you tie each knot. Continue to tie the lanyard knot for 16".

   The secret to tying a clean and smooth lanyard knot is patience in pulling each of the 6 cords in each group taut and straight before going on to the next knot. You will have to tug and pull all around the square lanyard knot several times before it is taut.

FIGURE 1
SQUARE LANYARD KNOT

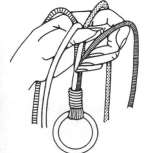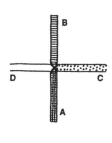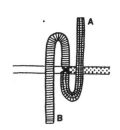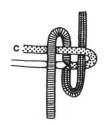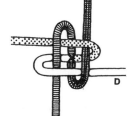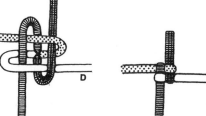

1. Same as step 1 for Chinese Crown Knot. Hold cords upside down in your hand *(or between your knees if that is easier)*.

2. Number the cords or groups of cords A - D as shown.

3. Fold Group A to the right & Group B to the left, parallel to each other forming 2 loops.

4. Thread Group C over & under as shown.

5. Thread Group D over & under as shown.

6. Pull each cord taut to form a tight square. Continue to tie the knot repeating steps 2 - 6. Always fold the groups of cords straight across the square.

5. Hang the ring from a high hook, from the ceiling, or from an over-the-door-hanger for easier knotting of the straps.

6. Work with one group of 6 cords to tie the first hanger strap:
   (a) Divide the cords into two groups of 3 cords each. Tie a square knot with each group of cords using 2 knotting cords around one center filler cord. This gives you 2 square knots in this row.

   (b) Alternate cords and tie a center square knot using 2 knotting cords around 2 filler cords.

   (c) Continue to tie this pattern of alternating square knots for 28", ending the sinnet with a single center square knot.

7. Repeat step 6 for each of the remaining groups of cords. You now have 4 completed straps of alternating square knots.

8. To connect the sinnets and form the cradle:
   (a) Drop down 6" from the end of the sinnets. Alternate cords, taking 3 cords from one sinnet plus 3 cords from the adjacent sinnet and tie a multiple 6-cord square knot using 4 knotting cords around 2 center filler cords. (See FIGURE 2)

   Repeat all the way around with each group of alternating 6 cords to begin forming the cradle.

   (b) Drop down 3" from the last row of multiple 6-cord-square-knots and tie another row of alternating multiple cord square knots, again using 4 knotting cords around 2 filler cords for each square knot.

   (c) Close the bottom of the cradle by tying a row of alternating 6-cord-square-knots next to the last row, again using 4 knotting cords around 2 filler cords for each square knot as before.

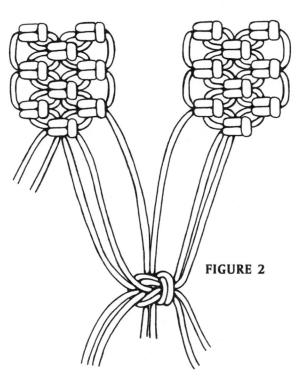

FIGURE 2

9. Cut a wrapping cord 2 yards long. Gather all tail cords together and wrap for 2" directly below the last row of square knots. Trim tail cords to desired length. To prevent the tail cords from unraveling, glue or fuse each cord end.

Double Doozy Hanger

Pictured on Page 51

> **Finished Length:** 6' 6" with tail cords
> *NOTE: If you want the finished hanger to be shorter, tie shorter sinnets.*
>
> ## SUPPLIES
> 6mm Braided Polypropylene Cord - 152 yards
>   (or 4-ply #72 Natural Jute Cord)
> 2" or 2 ½" soldered metal ring - 1

INSTRUCTIONS

1. CUT:
   12 Knotting Cords - 12 yards long
   1 Hanging Loop Wrapping Cord - 3 yards long

2. Use a scrap cord to tie the center of all 12 cords together. Measure 3" above the center and tie the end of the 3-yard loop wrapping cord around all 12 cords together. Continue to wrap all cords together for 6", untying the scrap cord when you come to it. Tie the end of the wrap cord to secure it in place. Trim loop wrap cord ends to 2" so they will be hidden in the gathering wrap.

3. Bend the wrapped cords to form a loop. Cut a new wrapping cord 2 ½ yards long. Insert the metal ring inside the loop. Gather all cords together, including the 2 short loop cord ends and tie a gathering wrap for 3". Trim both wrap cord ends close to the wrap.

4. Divide cords into 6 groups of 4 cords each. Bundle each group of cords with a rubber band to keep them from getting tangled in your working cords.

5. Working with one group of 4 cords, remove the rubber band and tie a half-knot-twist sinnet for 15" using 2 knotting cords around 2 filler cords, ending the sinnet with a square knot. Repeat for the remaining 5 groups of cords. You now have 6 half-knot-twist sinnets all around the hanger.

6. Connect all the sinnets and form the first cradle as follows:

   (a) Drop down 4" from the end of the half-knot-twist sinnets and tie a row of alternating square knots to connect the sinnets.

   (b) Drop down 2" from the last row of square knots and tie a row of alternating square knots.

   (c) Close the bottom of the cradle by tying a third row of alternating square knots up tight against the last row of knots.

7. Tie a row of square knot buttons around the bottom of the cradle as follows:

   (a) Alternate cords and tie a 6-square-knot sinnet with each group of 4 cords all around the hanger.

   (b) Form each button by threading the 2 filler cords through the space above the sinnet between the square knots in the previous row.

   (c) Tie an additional square knot under each button to hold it in place. This completes a row of square knot buttons around the bottom of the cradle.

8. Alternate cords and tie a second row of 6-square-knot buttons all the way around the hanger. Finish each button with a square knot to hold it in place.

9. Alternate cords again and tie a row of tight square knots up close to the last row of square knot buttons.

10. Alternate cords and use the 2 LONG knotting cords around the 2 SHORTER filler cords to tie a half-knot-twist sinnet that is 20" long with each group of 4 cords, ending with a square knot.

11. Repeat step 6 to complete the second cradle.

12. Repeat steps 7, 8 and 9 to tie the second set of alternating square knot buttons under the cradle.

13. Cut a wrapping cord 2 ½ yards long. Gather all cords together under the cradle and tie a 2" gathering wrap. Trim the top wrap cord close to the wrap. Trim tail cords 12" - 18" long or desired finished length. Fuse polypropylene cord ends to prevent unraveling. Glue jute cord ends.

Hanging Lace Hanger

Pictured on Back Cover

Finished Length: 4 ½' - 5' depending on tail cord length

SUPPLIES
3.5mm - 4mm Braided Polypropylene Cord - 85 yards
   (or 3-ply #28 Natural Jute Cord)
1 ½" or 2" soldered Metal Ring - 1

INSTRUCTIONS

1. CUT: 16 knotting cords - 5 yards long
          1 loop knotting cord - 3 yards long
          1 gathering wrap cord - 2 yards long

2. Use a scrap cord to tie the center of all 16 cords together. Pin this center to the knotting board. Slide the center of the 3-yard loop knotting cord underneath the 16 cords 3" above the center pins. Use the 2 short loop knotting cord ends to tie a square knot around the 16 filler cords at that point.

3. Repin cords to the knotting board through this square knot to the board. Untie the scrap cord. Continue to tie a 6" sinnet of square knots.

4. Remove cords from knotting board. Bend the square knot sinnet into a loop. Insert the metal ring inside the loop.

5. Gather all 32 cords together to close the loop. Use the 2 yard wrap cord to tie a 1 ½" gathering wrap around all 32 cords. Trim all loose short cords close to the wrap and fuse or glue to secure.

6. Divide cords into 4 groups of 8 cords each. Tie a multiple cord square knot with each group of cords up close to the wrap, using 4 knotting cords (2 on each side) around 4 center filler cords.

7. Working with the cords from one multiple cord square knot, divide these 8 cords into 2 groups of 4 cords each:

   (a) Tie a square knot with one group of 4 cords using 2 knotting cords around 2 center filler cords.

   (b) Drop down 1", exchange knotting cords and filler cords and tie a square knot with the 2 NEW knotting cords around the 2 NEW filler cords. (See FIGURE 1)

(c) Continue exchanging cords for each square knot, leaving a 1" space, until the sinnet is 28" long.

(d) Repeat steps (a) through (c) for the adjacent group of 4 cords from the first multiple cord square knot, to tie the second sinnet. You should now have 2 interchanging-square-knot sinnets side-by-side coming out of one multiple cord square knot at the beginning of the sinnets.

8. Repeat step 7 for each of the three remaining multiple cord square knots. You now have 8 interchanging square knot sinnets around the hanger.

9. To join all sinnets and form a cradle, tie a row of alternating square knots around the hanger next to the last knot in each sinnet.

10. Continue to tie 4 more rows of tight alternating square knots all around the hanger, forming a tube. *(If you are using #28 jute cord, tie 2 additional rows of tight alternating square knots, all around the hanger to form the tube.)*

11. Trim tail cords to 18" or desired finished length. Fuse polypropylene cords ends to prevent unraveling. Glue jute cord ends.

FIGURE 1
Exchange knotting cords & filler cords
to tie each square knot.

Buttons Hanger

Pictured on Back Cover

Finished Length: 4 ½ feet

SUPPLIES

3.5mm - 4mm Braided Polypropylene Cord - 93 yards
   (or 3-ply #28 Natural Jute Cord)
1 ½" or 2" Soldered Metal Ring - 1

INSTRUCTIONS

1. Cut: 8 knotting cords - 11 yards long
           1 loop knotting cord - 3 yards long

2. Use a scrap cord to tie the center of all 8 cords together. Pin this center to the knotting board.

3. Slide the center of the 3-yard loop knotting cord underneath all 8 cords 3" above the center pins. Use the 2 loop knotting cord ends to tie a square knot around all 8 filler cords at that point. Repin cords to the knotting board through this square knot. Untie the scrap cord. Continue to tie a 6" sinnet of square knots around the 8 cords.

4. Remove the cords from the knotting board. Bend the square knot sinnet into a loop. Insert the metal ring inside the loop.

5. Gather all 16 cords together to close the loop. Continue to use the same 2 short loop knotting cords to tie a 1" sinnet of square knots around all 16 cords. Trim the 2 short knotting cord ends and fuse or glue to secure.

6. Choose one of the following two methods for working with the cords as you form the square knot buttons according to the directions in step 7.

    (a) Use a large crochet hook to pull the cords through the small spaces between knots when forming the square knot buttons.

    (b) Or, fuse or glue the end of each cord to make it into a "needle" that will make it easier to thread the cords through the small spaces between knots while forming the square knot buttons.

        HINT: *When fusing polypropylene cord ends, I wet my fingers to keep from burning them and roll the melted cord ends into a needle point. You can use hot glue or white glue on jute cord ends. You will need to let the white glue dry before you can continue knotting.*

7. Divide cords into 4 groups of 4 cords each. Working with one group of 4 cords, tie a square knot button as follows:

   (a) Tie a square knot up close to the top square knot sinnet.

   (b) Leave a ¼" space and tie a sinnet of 10 square knots.

   (c) To form a square knot button, thread each center filler cord through the corresponding ¼" space and secure it with a tight square knot under the button.

   (d) Repeat this step for each of the remaining 3 groups of cords. You now have a row of square knot buttons around the hanger.

8. Alternate cords and tie a second row of square knot buttons, with 10 square knots in each button. To form each of these buttons, thread the 2 center filler cords together through the open space above the sinnet between 2 previous square knot buttons. Be sure to tie a tight square knot under the button to hold it in place.

9. Continue to tie three more rows of alternating 10-square-knot buttons for a total of 5 rows of buttons, ending each row with tight square knots to hold the buttons in place.

10. Tie a row of alternating square knots directly under the buttons.

11. Working with the 4 cords from one of the square knots just completed, tie the first hanger strap as follows:

    (a) Tie a 6" sinnet of square knots.

    (b) Leave a ¼" space and tie 5 square knots. To form a button, thread the center filler cords through the ¼" spaces.

    (c) **Exchange knotting cords and filler cords before you tie a tight square knot under the button to hold it in place.**

    (d) Continue to tie a 4" sinnet of square knots under the button.

    (e) Continue to alternate 5-square-knot-buttons and 4" square knot sinnets until you end with a fifth square knot button. Remember to always exchange knotting cords and filler cords before you tie each tight square knot under the button to hold it in place.

    (f) Repeat step 11 for the remaining 3 groups of cords to compete all 4 straps.

12. To connect all sinnets and form the cradle:

    (a) Drop down 5" and tie a row of alternating square knots around the hanger.

    (b) Drop down 2" and tie a second row of alternating square knots.

    (c) Tie a third row of alternating square knots next to the previous row of knots to close the bottom of the cradle

13. Cut a 2-yard wrapping cord. Gather all tail cords together and wrap for 2". Trim top wrap cord close to the wrap and fuse or glue to secure. Let the bottom end of the wrap cord hang with the tail cords. Trim tail cords to 12". Fuse polypropylene cords to prevent unraveling. Glue jute cord ends.

Picot Hanger

Pictured on Front Cover (see close-up of picots on page 51)

Finished Length: 5' 6"

SUPPLIES

6mm Braided Polypropylene Cord - 100 yards
  (or 4-ply #72 Natural Jute Cord)
1 ½" Soldered Metal Ring - 1

INSTRUCTIONS

1. Cut: 4 knotting cords - 9 yards long
      4 filler cords - 5 yards long
      1 loop knotting cord - 3 yards long

2. Use a scrap cord to tie the center of all 8 cords together. Pin this center to the knotting board.

3. Slide the center of the 3-yard loop knotting cord underneath all 8 cords 3" above the center pins. Use the 2 loop knotting cord ends to tie a square knot around all 8 filler cords at this point. Repin the cords to the knotting board through this square knot. Untie the scrap cord. Continue to tie a 6" sinnet of square knots around the 8 cords.

4. Remove cords from the knotting board. Bend the square knot sinnet into a loop. Insert the metal ring inside the loop.

5. Gather all 16 cords together to close the loop. Continue to use the same 2 short loop knotting cords to tie a 1" sinnet of square knots around all 16 cords together. Trim the 2 short knotting cord ends and fuse or glue to secure.

6. Divide cords into 4 groups of 4 cords each with 2 long knotting cords and 2 short filler cords in each group.

7. Working with one group of 4 cords, tie one hanger strap as follows:

    (a) Use the 2 long knotting cords around the 2 short filler cords and tie a 20" square knot sinnet.

    (b) Drop down 2" and tie a square knot. Push this knot up close to the previous knot to form a square knot picot. Tie another square knot next to the picot.

    (c) Drop down 3" and tie a square knot. Push this knot up close to the previous knot to form a second larger square knot picot. Tie another square knot next to the picot.

    (d) Drop down 2" and tie a square knot. Push this knot up close to the previous knot to form a third square knot picot equal in size to the first picot. Tie another square knot next to the picot.

(e) Cut 2 new knotting cords that are each 5 yards long. Divide the 4 cords from this sinnet into 2 groups of 2 filler cords each. Fold one of the new cords in half and add it to 2 of the filler cords with a square knot. Continue to tie a 10" sinnet of square knots.

Repeat to add the second new 5-yard cord to the other 2 filler cords in this strap, tying a second square knot sinnet 10" long.

8. Repeat step 7 for each of the remaining three groups of cords to complete 4 double straps for the hanger.

9. To connect all sinnets and form the cradle:

(a) Drop down 4" from the end of the square knot sinnets and tie a row of alternating square knots to connect the sinnets and begin to form the cradle.

(b) Drop down 2" from the last row of square knots and tie a row of alternating square knots.

(c) Close the bottom of the cradle by tying a third row of square knots up tight against the last row of knots.

10. Cut a wrapping cord 1 yard long. Gather all the tail cords together under the cradle and tie a gathering wrap for 1". Trim both short wrap cord ends close to the wrap and fuse or glue to secure. Trim tail cords to 12" - 18" or desired length. Fuse or glue each cord end to prevent unraveling.

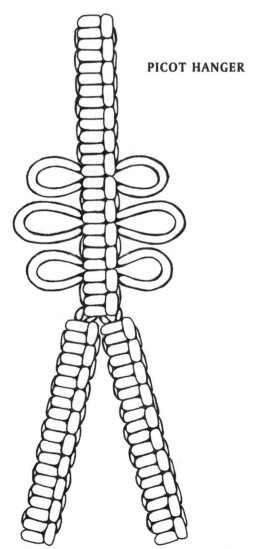

PICOT HANGER

Open Spaces Hanger

Pictured on Page 51

Finished Length: 6 feet

SUPPLIES

6mm Braided Polypropylene Cord - 96 yards
   (or 4-ply #72 Natural Jute Cord)
2" or 2 ½" Soldered Metal Ring - 1

INSTRUCTIONS

1. CUT: 4 knotting cords - 16 yards long
           4 filler cords - 6 yards long
           1 loop knotting cord - 5 yards long

2. Use a scrap cord to tie the center of all 8 cords together. Pin this center to the knotting board.

3. Slide the center of the 5-yard loop knotting cord under all 8 cords 3" above the center pins.
    Use the 2 knotting cord ends to tie a square knot around all 8 filler cords. Unpin the center pins
    and repin the cords to the board through this square knot. Continue to tie a 6" sinnet of square
    knots around the 8 filler cords.

4. Remove cords from the board. Bend the sinnet into a loop. Insert the metal ring into the loop.

5. Gather all 16 cords together to close the loop. Continue to use the 2 loop knotting cord ends to
    tie a 4" half-knot-twist sinnet around all 16 cords. Trim each short cord close to the last half
    knot and fuse or glue to secure.

6. Divide cords into 4 groups of 4 cords each with 2 long knotting cords and 2 short filler cords in
    each group. Tie a square knot with each group of 4 cords using 2 long knotting cords around 2
    short filler cords.

7. To tie one sinnet strap:

    (a) Working with one group of 4 cords, tie 12 half knots to form a half-knot-twist sinnet.

    (b) Tie 1 square knot. Number cords 1-4 from the left to the right.
        Use cord 2 as the anchor cord and cord 1 as the knotting cord and tie 5 left-hand vertical
        lark's head knots. Then use cord 3 as the anchor cord and cord 4 as the knotting cord and tie
        5 right-hand vertical lark's head knots. (See FIGURE 1) Tie a square knot to connect both
        vertical lark's head sinnets forming an oval.

    (c) Tie a 12-half-knot-twist sinnet using all 4 cords.

(d) Repeat steps (b) and (c) four more times, ending with a square knot to complete one hanger strap sinnet.

8. Repeat step 7 for each of the 3 remaining groups of 4 cords to complete 4 sinnets.

9. To form the cradle, drop down 6" alternate cords and tie 2 square knots with each group of 4 cords.

10. Drop down 3" alternate cords and tie 2 square knots with each group of 4 cords.

11. Close the bottom of the cradle by tying a row of alternating square knots up close to the previous row.

12. Cut a knotting cord 4 yards long. Gather all 16 tail cords together. Center the knotting cord behind the tail cords and tie a half knot. Continue to tie a half-knot-twist-sinnet 3" long.

13. Trim the 2 knotting cords close to the last half knot and fuse or glue to secure. Trim tail cords to 18". Fuse, glue or knot each tail cord to prevent unraveling.

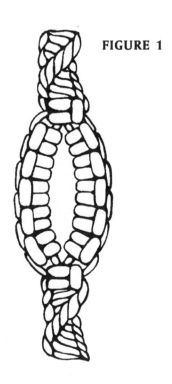 **FIGURE 1**

Majestic Hanging Table

Pictured on Front Cover (also see close-up photos on page 51)

Finished Length: 7 feet (including tail cords)

SUPPLIES

3-Ply #72 Natural Jute Cord - 290 yards
  (or 6mm Braided Polypropylene Cord)
2" or 2 ½" Soldered Metal Ring - 1
5" Soldered Metal Rings - 2
19" diameter glass circle
  (Available at minimal expense at many discount & home
  improvement stores - sold separately to accompany a 3-legged
  wood table. Also can be purchased from a glass company.)

INSTRUCTIONS

1. CUT: 8 knotting cords - 22 yards long
          8 knotting cords - 13 yards long
          1 loop knotting cord - 5 yards long

   Use a scrap cord to tie the center of all 16 long cords together. Pin the center to the knotting board.

2. Slide the center of the loop knotting cord underneath all 16 cords 4" above the center pins. Use the 2 loop knotting cord ends to tie a square knot around all 16 cords at this point. Repin this square knot to the knotting board. Continue to tie an 8" sinnet of square knots around the 16 filler cords.

3. Cut a new wrapping cord 2 yards long. Remove cords from the board. Bend the sinnet into a loop. Insert the 2 ½" ring into the loop.

4. Gather all 32 knotting cords together to close the loop, including the 2 short loop knotting cord ends, and wrap for 2". Trim all 4 short cord ends *(2 from the loop and 2 from the wrap)* close to the wrap. Fuse or glue these cord ends to secure.

5. Hang the ring from a ceiling hook or an over-the-door-hanger to finish tying the hanging table. Divide all cords into 8 groups of 4 cords each, with 2 long knotting cords and 2 short filler cords in each group. Use a scrap cord or rubber band to bundle each group together temporarily.

6. Working with one group of 4 cords, tie a 6" half-knot-twist sinnet using the 2 long knotting cords around the 2 shorter filler cords. Repeat for each group of 4 cords around the hanger. You now have 8 half-knot-twist sinnets.

7. Place all cords down through one 5" metal ring. Mount the cords onto the ring as follows. Because the diameter of cords vary, you may have to adjust whether you double half hitch or triple half hitch the cords onto the ring:

    (a) Working with one sinnet, double half hitch the 2 center short filler cords side-by-side onto the ring. Triple half hitch each outside long knotting cord from the same sinnet onto the ring on each side of the short cords. Then go to the opposite side of the ring and repeat this step to attach those 4 cords from the opposite sinnet, mounting them onto the ring in the same manner. Make sure the ring is level and steady.

    (b) Select a middle sinnet between the ones already on the ring and repeat for mounting those cords onto the ring. Then go to the opposite side and mount that sinnet onto the ring in the same manner. You now have 4 sinnets mounted onto the ring, spaced evenly around the ring.

    (c) Continue to mount the remaining sinnets onto the ring in the same manner.

8. Alternate cords from the sinnets and tie a row of square knots under the ring, using 2 short knotting cords around 2 long filler cords for each square knot.

9. Alternate cords again and tie a row of square knot buttons as follows:

    (a) Working with one group of 4 cords, tie a sinnet of 6 square knots.

    (b) To form each button, thread the 2 center filler cords through the open space between the square knots in the previous row to form the button.

    (c) Tie a tight square knot under the button to hold it in place.

10. Tie 4 more rows of alternating square knot buttons, with 6 square knots in each button. Always finish with a square knot to hold the button in place.

11. Tie a row of alternating square knots up close to the last row of buttons.

12. Repeat Step 7 to mount all cords onto the second 5" metal ring, working on opposite sides as before.

13. Alternate cords under the ring and tie a single row of half knots using 2 long knotting cords around 2 shorter filler cords for each half knot next to the ring.

14. To tie one hanger strap:

    (a) Working with one group of 4 cords, continue to tie a 5" half-knot-twist sinnet using the 2 long knotting cords around the 2 shorter filler cords. Repeat for the adjoining group of cords. You now have two side-by-side half-knot-twist sinnets.

    (b) Tie a square knot with the 4 center cords to connect the two sinnets. (See FIGURE 1 on page 48)

    (c) Alternate cords and tie a row of 2 square knots.

    (d) Tie a square knot with the 4 center cords.

    (e) Repeat steps (a) through (d) 6 more times.

(f) Finish the strap by tying a 6" half-knot-twist sinnet with each of the 2 groups of 4 cords.

15. Repeat step 14 three more times to complete the four straps of the hanging table.

16. To form the cradle that will hold the glass circle, follow FIGURE 2:

   (a) Number the 8 cords from each double sinnet strap 1 through 8 from the left to the right (1-4 cords in left-hand sinnet and cords 5-8 in right-hand sinnet). Tie a square knot with cords 7-8 from one double strap sinnet and cords 1-2 from the adjacent double strap sinnet to the right to connect these two straps, creating a new alternating group of 8 cords.

   (b) Tie 3 more rows of alternating square knots with this new group of 8 cords, ending with a row of 2 square knots.

   (c) Repeat this method of connecting straps as you work your way around the hanger, alternating the cords from one double sinnet strap with the cords from an adjacent double sinnet strap.

17. Alternate cords and tie a row of square knots all the way around the hanger, connecting all cords and forming a tube.

18. Cut a wrapping cord 3 yards long. Gather all cords together and tie a 2" gathering wrap. Trim the top wrap cord close to the wrap and fuse or glue to secure. The bottom wrap cord will hang with the tail cords. Trim tail cords 12" - 18".   Fuse or glue all cord ends to prevent unraveling.

   Insert glass circle into the cradle. Hang and enjoy!

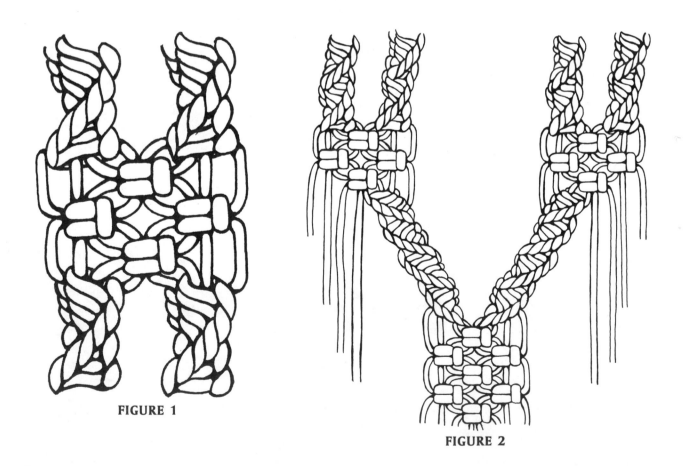

FIGURE 1

FIGURE 2

Memories Frame

A Bonus Project reprinted from Judy Palmer's <u>Macramé For Today</u> (no longer in print)

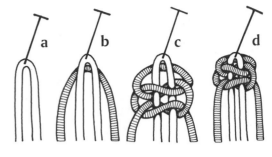

FIGURE 1

SUPPLIES

3-Ply #28 Natural Jute Cord - 16 yards
(or 3.5 - 4mm Braided Polypropylene Cord)
Paper Maché Picture Frame
5" x 7" outside dimensions, 3 ½" x 5" photo size
Hot glue & glue gun

OPTIONAL: Acrylic Paint to match Polypropylene Cord
Paint Brush

INSTRUCTIONS

IMPORTANT: Lay your sinnets on the frame before cutting as the size of your frame may vary from the one I used.

1. Paint the frame to match the color of cord you are using. Set aside to dry.

2. Cut: 4 filler cords - 12" long
   4 knotting cords - 1 ⅓ yards long

3. Fold one filler cord in half and pin the center to the macramé board. Fold one knotting cord in half and add it to the filler cords with a tight square knot up next to the pins (see FIGURE 1).

4. Tie a 3 ¾" sinnet of square knots. Trim all 4 cords close to the last square knot and fuse or glue cord ends to secure.

5. Repeat steps 3 & 4 three more times for a total of 4 short square knot sinnets. Set all sinnets aside.

6. Cut: 4 filler cords - 18" long
   4 knotting cords - 1 yard, 30" long

7. Fold one filler cord in half and pin the center to the macramé board. Fold one knotting cord in half and add it to the filler cords with a tight square knot up next to the pins (see FIGURE 1).

8. Tie a 5 ¾" sinnet of square knots. Trim all 4 cords close to the last square knot and fuse or glue cord ends to secure.

9. Repeat steps 7 & 8 three more times for total of 4 longer square knot sinnets.

10. Glue 2 rows of sinnets side by side to the frame as shown in FIGURE 2.

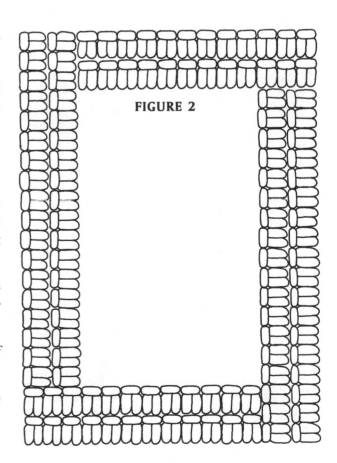

FIGURE 2

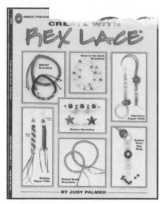

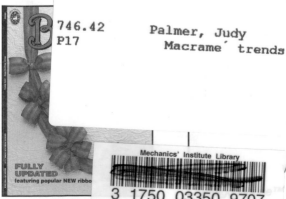